THE WHITE DOVE

JANE CANDIA COLEMAN

HIGH PLAINS PRESS

Poetry of the American West Series

Cover photograph © by Helga Teiwes

FIRST PRINTING

1 3 5 7 9 8 6 4 2

*The Wyoming bucking horse and rider trademark
is federally registered by the State of Wyoming
and is licensed for restricted use through the Secretary of State's office.*

Library of Congress Cataloging-in-Publication Data

Coleman, Jane Candia
The White Dove / Jane Candia Coleman.
p. cm. -- (Poetry of the American West)
ISBN-13: 978-0-931271-83-0 (pbk. : alk. paper)
ISBN-10: 0-931271-83-5 (pbk. : alk. paper)
1. Kino, Eusebio Francisco, 1644-1711--Poetry.
2. West (U.S.)--Poetry.
I. Title.
II. Series.
PS3553.047427W48 2007
811'.54--dc22
2006004508

HIGH PLAINS PRESS
403 Cassa Road
Glendo, WY 82213
1-800-552-7819

Catalog available.
www.highplainspress.com

THE
WHITE

DOVE

Jane Candia Coleman

Dedicated to Father Eusebio Kino, S.J.
and his legacy.

❧ CONTENTS

Fill your eyes, your mind,
your heart with visible and invisible light.
❧ Teilhard de Chardin, S.J.

❧ PREFACE

It is almost forty years since I saw Segno, the small town in the Italian Alps where Eusebio Kino was born in 1645. Even then I knew who he was—one of the Jesuit missionaries who had brought Christianity to Mexico and the Southwest, but at the time it was the landscape that fascinated me—the mountains dominating the sky, a road that curved and twisted back upon itself in perilous descent, and on the slopes of the valley what I thought were apple trees in full, fluttering bloom.

Without knowing it, I then followed Kino's early path to learning and the priesthood—out of Segno to Trento and the Jesuit school, then north to Bolzano, Bressanone, the Brenner Pass into Austria. It was the route Hannibal, his army, and his elephants had taken centuries before, and Kino had followed it to the Jesuit Colleges in Austria and Bavaria.

Neither did I know that little more than a year later I would see for the first time the church of San Xavier del Bac, the White Dove of the Desert, for which Kino laid the cornerstones, and that I would stand spellbound, wordless, touched—perhaps, by Kino himself—with wonder at its beauty.

It was sunset. The sky flamed orange, scarlet, gold, a lily unfolding, a cascade of fire that radiated from the white walls of the church so that it shimmered and seemed less a part of earth than of heaven, a reliquary containing echoes of an extraordinary past.

I carried away with me a vision that has never left, a fleeting glimpse into history, a feeling of kinship with those who had labored here in the seventeenth and eighteenth centuries and who loved this desert country and its people as I do.

Fourteen years passed. It was Christmas Eve, and I was driving back to Tucson after a day spent exploring the border country on horseback. It was just after sunset, and the road was almost deserted, the sky to the west a dull bronze against which mountains hunched in black relief.

In the distance, lights glimmered, hundreds of them like fireflies hovering in mid-air. Coming closer, I saw *luminarias* lining the walls, the roof and bell tower of the Tumacacori Mission, and I was struck again by the beauty of ancient tradition, by the sweet simplicity of the celebration of the birth of Christ, not only here but in towns and villages across the Southwest and Mexico. Here was the truth Father Kino and so many others had brought, a truth now interwoven with native culture and all the more beautiful for it.

"Come," the little lamps urged. "Come and be joyful."

Inside the ancient mission walls, a boys' choir was singing, and the purity of their voices seemed another echo of the past, of the days when Tumacacori had been a thriving mission, a stopping place for Kino on his way to other missions and explorations of a land that had never been mapped or charted, but one for which he felt a deep love and a driving curiosity to explore; the days when there were lush fields and citrus groves planted by the missionaries and watered by the Santa Cruz River. There had been singing then, too—a choir of native boys struggling with Gregorian Chant and the words of the Latin mass—the music of crude violins, wood drums, flutes fashioned from the reeds that grew at water's edge.

Alone, I wandered into the mission garden, knowing that three hundred years before the priests had planted and tended a similar plot of herbs, fruit, vegetables. Is not a garden a place of worship as well as sustenance? And did they not, perhaps, wander the paths as I was doing, breviaries in hand, the Angelus, the Psalms on their lips? It has been written that when Kino read the prayers in his missal, he wept, and when, in the clear, cold air the notes of far-away carols fell around me like snowflakes, I understood his emotions.

I walked, naming the herbs like a chant—mint, oregano, sage, a rosemary high as my shoulder and covered with blue flowers, the color, so legend has it, of the Virgin's cloak. A touch released its fragrance, sharp, resinous like so many plants of arid countries, and I plucked one sprig for remembrance, carried it away with me as I carried the essence of that magical Eve.

Was it then that Father Kino, his life, his accomplishments took hold of me? Or had it begun in Segno, where the River Noce, swollen with snow-melt, races down to join the Adige, and in spring the orchards fling petals across the Val di Non? Or was it the day when I wrote my first "Kino" poem, a gift, perhaps, from the Father, himself, for certainly, as I began to visualize a book on his life, many of the poems came as if dictated, poems unlike any I had ever written or had thought to write.

Others came harder. These poems made demands, forced me to question, to do research, to travel, to stretch my mind beyond its limits. These were poems that did not permit easy satisfaction, not in one revision nor in twenty. I labored for precision, for poems that not only were logical and coherent but that, I hoped, might be a reflection of Kino, himself. Kino the explorer, the mathematician and cartographer, the astronomer, linguist, breeder of cattle and fine Spanish Barb horses. Kino the philosopher. The priest. A many-faceted man of keen intelligence and extraordinary energy. An aesthetic who refused salt on his food, drank bitter herbs, and who, in his constant and arduous travels, slept, if he did, on the ground, his saddle as pillow, his horse's blanket as cover.

What his thoughts were, no one can know, not even reading through his extensive diaries that covered his years in what became know as the Pimeria Alta, the Land of the Upper Pimas.

And to understand the enormity of his accomplishments, they must be placed in the context of his time.

Eusebio Kino arrived in Mexico in 1681, almost one hundred years before the start of the American Revolution, and two hundred years before the Gunfight at the O.K. Corral put its nefarious mark on Arizona history. What he found was a vast, often violent and inhospitable country, for the most part unexplored, the native people primitive and superstitious.

In the Europe he left behind, it was the beginning of the Age of Enlightenment, the era of the Baroque. As mathematician and astronomer, Kino had certainly studied the theories of Galileo, Copernicus, Kepler, Newton, and Tycho Brahe (the Dane of the silver nose). As priest he knew the philosophical works of Descartes and Spinoza, and in various churches, schools, and courts had heard the music of Buxtehude, Monteverdi, possibly Purcell and Cavalli. Bernini was at work on the Church of Saint Peter in Rome, and in London Christopher Wren was designing Saint Paul's. Rembrandt and Reubens were the painters of the age, and Vermeer and his Dutch contemporaries were re-creating the light and shadows, the interiors of houses and churches of the Low Countries. Louis XIV was on the throne of France, Charles the Second was scandalizing England, and in Rome Innocent XI was Pope.

Faced with unimaginable and unforeseen difficulties, the young Eusebio Kino embraced his new land, his task as missionary with customary zeal. Though his dream had always been to be sent to China, a chance he had lost by a drawing of straws with a fellow priest, he accepted his posting with good grace and, possibly, with a touch of humor, and when he died in 1711, he left behind an extraordinary legacy, much of which, in the form of mission towns and churches, remains today.

It must be noted that the present San Xavier del Bac Mission was built by the Franciscans who followed the Jesuits into Mexico and Arizona. The accepted dates for its construction are 1783–1797. Father Juan Bautista Velderrain raised the money and oversaw the project until his death in 1790. His successor, Father Juan Bausta Llorens completed the construction. Yet it was Kino who blazed the trail, laid the cornerstones, and, I like to think, envisioned the Mission as it is today.

One last note. Father Kino was baptized in Segno in 1645 as Eusebius Chinus or Chino. Since then the name has gone through many modifications, including the one Kino gave himself and by which he is known, Chino being Spanish for Chinese. The current Italian spelling is Chini.

What I have attempted here may be only my own vision, try though I have to capture the man, devoted as I have been to a task that, over many years, developed into a vocation. Only Father Kino, himself, knows if I have succeeded.

           Jane Candia Coleman

ꙮ Acknowledgments

I am grateful to all those who believed in me during the years it took to bring Father Kino and his era to life. My husband, historian Glenn Boyer, urged me on and gave me his unqualified support and suggestions. The poet Victoria Tester offered encouragement and shared my joy as each new poem appeared. Jon Tuska of the Golden West Agency prevented me from making errors in Latin. My sincere thanks to Dr. Bernard Fontana who answered my questions about dates and names swiftly and succinctly, and who suggested that I contact the extraordinary photographer, Helga Teiwes. Her photo of the San Xavier Mission in moonlight is, to me, the perfect jacket cover. I owe thanks to Nancy Curtis of High Plains Press, who years ago understood what I was attempting to do—bring the American West and its diverse people and history to life through poetry. New friends Arlene and Ken Svilich sent me to the DeGrazia Gallery of the Sun to see the haunting paintings of Kino's life and the joyful and unusual Kino chapel there, and introduced me to William R. Stoeger, S.J. whose wise advice and understanding of the creative process sent me down new and productive paths. Father Stoeger has been the good angel for this book, and I owe him my unending gratitude. Lastly, I thank Father Kino, himself, who it seemed was there guiding me and, when I despaired, said, "Keep on."

PART ONE
1678–1685

FAREWELL
Genoa, Italy, June, 1678

A tree ripped from its earth
cries out, as does a child
taken from its mother.
Europe recedes
behind a curtain of cloud,
and with it youth,
my mother's face awash in tears.

Though my heart aches,
my soul flies free
like the ship beneath me,
its tattered sails brought to life
with a sweep of wind's tongue.

Kino... Kino...
Who is it calls my name?
What voice is it I hear
balanced in the bow
and looking out across
the blue arms of the sea?

I know. My answer's clear.
I come, I come, wither I am taken.
Memory sustains, and fervor drives.
Oh, let Thy will be done.

VERONICA'S VEIL
Alicante, Spain, 1678

One must kneel before this blood-stained cloth,
this blessed countenance, and kneel in silence,
for, in truth, no prayer suffices.
His agony made visible becomes my own,
obliterating childish dreams of martyrdom.

Before this miracle, I am become nothing,
a reed shaken, a puny voice trapped in flesh,
all vision shattered as glass is shattered
into shards and dust, for dust I am.

Master. Lord. The words are thought only,
a light within that blinds me to all else.
Gladly will I give my life if so required.
Joyously will I share His crown of thorns,
bear the heavy cross upon my shoulders,
go where I am called.

Beyond these church walls, small sparrows
are lifted into air as random leaves
are lifted, tossed at the wind's dictate,
as once again I give myself into His service.

———————————

On the way to the new world from Italy, Kino's ship, The Capitana, *stopped in Alicante, Spain, where there was a Jesuit college. Kino and his fellow Jesuits stayed a week and visited, among other places, the monastery of Saint Veronica where the miraculous veil, thought to be imprinted with the face of Christ, was kept.*

THE WHITE DOVE

SUNDIAL
Seville, Spain

To make a sundial
one must observe the sun—
its position, angle, shadow
cast without regard to weather.

One must take a stone
and smooth its surface,
sculpt the gnomon
shaped like a single wing,

an occupation demanding patience
and a knowledge of the skies
and planets that even now
is better left unspoken.

So my hands labor
while intellect mocks
superstition.
Earth turns, spinning.
The sun's immovable.

(continued)

No heresy in this.
No crime. Galileo did penance
for us all. Still, I remain mute,
fashioning the stones,
the pace of hours
and the speech of days,
marking the hypocrisy of time.

Because of a navigational error and erratic winds, Kino's ship, The Capitana, arrived in Cadiz just in time to miss the Spanish fleet that was to carry the priests to Mexico. They stayed in Seville for almost two years awaiting another fleet, and while there, Father Kino and the others busied themselves in preparation for their missionary work. Some studied mathematics and astronomy, others labored with their hands. Kino, according to a letter written by Father Ratkay, his associate, built at least one sundial. His mention of Galileo refers to Galileo's trial by the Inquisition in which he was forced to recant his support of the Copernican theory that the sun is stationary and the earth revolves around it.

THE WHITE DOVE

ANNUNCIATION
Seville, Spain

> *All creation brings with it,*
> *as its accompanying risk and shadow, some fault.*
> Teilhard de Chardin, S.J.

Morning carries the scent of rain,
and in the old bed, where sweet grass
grows high as my knees, white iris
are blooming. They are graceful
as the sculpted hands of saints,
white as marble and frightening
in their purity.

Nothing in this world is without stain
if one believes in sin. Even the newborn
come cursed, their first crying
an appeal for mercy.

If there is justice in this
I cannot find it, though I kneel
in the moist earth and reach out
to these pale messengers,
these simple beings
that have never questioned innocence
or begged forgiveness for their birth.

A LETTER

Chacala, Mexico, 1682

Tomorrow begins our voyage
from Mexico to the Californias.

We have three ships.
They tug at anchor
as eager to be off
as horses facing the wind.

Though once I dreamed of China,
as you know, my reality is here
in a country not unlike yours,

with its mountains,
deserts, and the sea
that lures as the Sirens
lured brave Odysseus.

Yet how huge the chasm
between this new world and that.
How useless all my studies
of equations and the stars!

Here's emptiness and distance
unimagined, the politics and jealousies
of the small. Here my only symbols
will be the simple act of prayer,
the baptizing of those who come
in hope.

Tomorrow I go—priest, soldier—
armed only with belief and fortitude,
the holy image of the Virgin
you so kindly gave to me.

The wind is rising.
Clouds extinguish stars.
How black the night becomes!
As it was in the beginning

when darkness
was upon the face of the deep.

It was while Kino was in Spain awaiting passage to Mexico that he
began a correspondence with Maria Guadalupe de Lancaster, Duchess
of Aveiro, Arcos y Maqueda, and a descendant of John of Gaunt.
Originally, Kino hoped that the Duchess, a supporter of the Jesuits in
the Orient, would help him in his quest to be sent to China, but as time
went on, a friendship that was to last for many years sprang up
between them. Just before Kino left Spain, the Duchess sent him a
painting of "Mary Mother of God and crowned with stars." This poem,
in the form of a letter, is, of course, from my own imagination. Letters
from Father Kino to the Duchess are in the Huntington Library.

IN SEARCH OF PEARLS
Baja, California, 1683

Atondo, our Captain, paws through shells
exclaiming over pearls no larger
than withered grapes, misshapen lentils.
He believes he will discover riches
for himself, the church, the King of Spain
as did Coronado with his dreams of Cibola—
both incongruous in this fragile paradise
where desert marries sea and is content.

For thus must paradise have been—
untouched, existing for itself and for those two
whose innocence was doomed to fail.
And we men come bringing greed
and Christianity, greed's antithesis.

No pearl's as precious as a single soul,
and worldly wealth cannot erase perfection—
how the sun strikes gold into each wave's heart.
How whales, those gentle monsters
so unlike myth, rise up gleaming
from the depths and play like children,
give birth and nurture as all mothers do.
Are even these not blessed, worth more
than all mankind's puny and disastrous hungers?

The tide laps at my feet, its motion heaven's dictate.
I would have the treasures of the sea remain inviolate,
as when the spirit of God first moved upon the waters.

Captain Isidro Atondo had been appointed by the Spanish to make yet another attempt to colonize the California peninsula. As was common practice, two missionaries accompanied the expedition—Father Eusebio Kino and Father Mathias Goni. The captain and his men spent much time searching for pearls. The two missionaries labored to communicate with the native Indians and to set up a camp and a mission. Eventually, due to the native's distrust combined with a lack of rainfall, the endeavor failed.

MAP MAKING

The sea's at our backs.
My tired mule stops at hill's crest,
and together we look out at endless
desert beneath endless sky.

Ocotillo writes its thin, black script
upon the sand, a language
as unintelligible as my own darkness,
transmitting the sharp definition
between life and death,
the terrifying chasm of the soul.

Who would come here
without intervention?
What lunatic or fool
attempts to chart the reach
of mountain, sky, self?

Only I, Kino, on no more
than a gamble, a drawing
of two straws, the prize
the Orient, this barrenness
to the loser.

And so I come, with faith
heavy upon me,
into this land beyond word,
or thought, or any map
devised by man's assumption.

Into this empty, fragile place
so like ourselves.
This place that breaks the heart
then mends it with indifference.

---

*Upon leaving Italy, Kino had drawn straws with his fellow Jesuit,
Antonio Kerschpamer, to decide which of them would go to the Orient
and which to Mexico. Kino, as we know, lost the draw.*

MIRAGE

Enter this web of canyons
at your own risk.
Wander the labyrinth
of vanished rivers
crumbling faults,

and somewhere you
will meet yourself
pared to the bone,
as the bones underfoot
will testify.

These painted hills
thrusting out of earth,
these barren trails
do not lie except
with permission.

No falseness here,
only the double edge
of truth—peril
or perfection.
Choose one or both
with caution,

for the eye's a tricky thing
and hope deceives.
Reach out for water,
crimson rock,
the slice of wings
against the heart of sky

and grasp the emptiness of air,
the whitened grimace
of illusion.

THEREFORE I AM

> *If I should lose all faith in God,*
> *I think that I should continue to believe invincibly in the world.*
>   Teilhard de Chardin

Why, here also is music!
The rest between notes,
the interminable breath
between sound and sound.

Is not silence
as much a language
as any other
and filled with possibility?

As when God, enthroned
in thunderous silence
looked upon a void
and knew these stones
still warm beneath my hand
though it be night,

the cactus crowned with blossom,
the music of the wind
upon the perfectly created
swirling of my ear.

Doubting, I doubt not.
In this desert place
who can question what they know
or, thinking, have believed?

In silence is beginning and end
and beginning again. As it was
and shall be. In *saecula, saeculorum.*

OFFERTORY

He is many-colored,
startling in his swiftness,
this lizard that darts across the altar.
He is seen, then unseen
like the edges of thought.

As I offer the Host
I am silenced
by the incongruity,
the simple trust
of all things living,
even as I celebrate
the Word made flesh.

Halted in the act of prayer,
I ponder for one moment
the universality
of gesture, action, belief.

Tell me, I say to both
creature and Creator,
*Tell me for whom miracles
happen. Tell me that even the smallest
are blessed, and that I may indulge
in delight at the sight of one quick,
flickering lizard upon this humble altar.*

QUESTION

What matters, it seems,
are the least, the fragile lilies
of the field, the ubiquitous sparrows,
the unwanted infants born of ignorance.

What matters is love
or, perhaps, compassion,
the overflowing
of our hearts, a tenderness

God-given, the hope
that even the least
may survive and triumph,
that even a gilded moth

dancing around a flame
might have a duty
we cannot know.
After all, who are we?

PART TWO

1687–1700

ANGELUS

My voice shalt thou hear in the morning, oh Lord.
Psalm 5

It is the hour of rejoicing
when night becomes day,
the hour of the first prayer,
and yet the ancient words
are vanquished by the sight
of ocotillo against yellow sky.

Words die before birth.
There is no language known
to speak of what might be called
desire, or ecstasy, or simple madness.

Am I mad, then, for reaching out
in silence like any pagan of my flock
to cup the rising sun
and worship light?

Am I mad, or is prayer simply happiness,
unity with world and circumstance,
a fragile thread connecting life
with life, the hope of immortality?

The Jesuit Teilhard de Chardin wrote of saying his solitary daily mass on the steppes of Mongolia—"I have neither bread, nor wine, nor altar. I shall rise beyond symbols to the pure majesty of the real, and I shall offer you ... on the altar of the whole earth, the toil and sorrow of the world."

AND STILL IT MOVES

The small pond holds the moon on its face,
reflection of reflection, sun and moon
together without dissent.

In this moment, in this solitary place
lit by the double light of heaven,
there are no voices, accusations,
judgments brought down
upon innocent seekers of truth.

For those who would sway common beliefs,
there is only struggle against a world
well-versed in evil's ignorance.

E pur si move.
Galileo's words echo between mountains.
Still, it moves—this earth
this spinning globe
this star-mottled sky.

Galileo, who, through his fractured glass,
changed all and suffered for it,
locked not in a cell
but in the chambers of his mind,
as I am locked within the cage
of my belief, my vows, my determined course
among a people who, in their innocence,
have no need of me.

I believe, but doubt lives in us all,
a duality as the moon is other,
as I, so filled with argument,
face a thousand disbelievers
and question self, reason, faith.
I, who with a single gesture,
can shatter a perfect mirror.

FALSE GODS

Who could have foreseen the love I bear
for a country not my own? A love
that's almost greater than that I owe
to Him who set my feet upon a path
unwanted and unknown.

The voice of conscience tells me
I should suffer guilt because
this desert place of sand and bones
and beauty has brought me to my knees
in adoration. I, Kino, whose loyalty
has always been to God, Christ, the Trinity.

Mea culpa. Mea culpa
I beg forgiveness for a sin I cannot help.
In this I'm like the flocks I tend,
those innocents who worship multitudes
of gods and in their simple way
are not mistaken, for He lives within all things.

I am forced to worship the frailty
of a thousand lives, the blessedness
of rain and thunder clouds, a land
where everything seems sacred
is, in itself, miraculous.

I came bringing beads and faith,
olive trees and wheat, herds of cattle,
sheep, horses to those whose history
predates intellect, their prayers
as meaningful to them as rain
baptizing scented earth.

If it were possible, I would take all
in my hands—mountains, sky, the lilies
of the fields, those radiant chalices
wrought in gold—and make an offering
to the Creator, a giving back of love,
and sacrifice, and gratitude, a small
most humble prayer rising like the dust
in heat-struck, perfect timelessness.

SONORA SPRING

1.

Like Pentecostal tongues of flame,
these wind-spurred poppies
reflect heaven's radiance
freely given.

Their petals lie cool in my hand,
the same as those that light the valley,
blaze across the mountain's face
consuming nothing,

proof that fire can be
both hot and cold,
so that, I think, the fires of hell
might only be the heat of unfulfilled desire
in infinite and torturous repetition.

2.

And after these, the cactus
crowns its head with white,
undisputed Queen of May,
sweet source of fruit and wine.

Here, even the thorniest
give sustenance and cause
for rejoicing,
as the women's' baskets—
woven with such patience
from dry grass and willow bark—
fill now with nature's jewels.

Each a sacred vessel.
Chalice.
Holiest of Grails.

(continued)

3.

Around me the Pimas are dancing.
Frenzied, they purge themselves,
an orgy born of a thousand years
spent worshipping elusive rain.

Drink! Drink!
Wine the color of blood spills
from an offered *olla*
and I dare not refuse,
for who am I to turn away
from ritual and belief?.

I've heard the ploughmen chanting
in their fields, watched fishermen
float candles on the sea
to placate ancient gods.
Abraham prepared for sacrifice,
and each day I take Christ's blood
in thanks and celebration.

Who's to say what prayers
will be denied or answered?
God is in all things, all hearts.
I cannot refuse this cup
He offers me.

LAS GOLONDRINAS

On the *vigas* of Mission Dolores
swallows sit on mud nests.
How patient they are, these tiny birds
colored blue, rust, a flash of apricot!

How they persevere
in building the birth place,
rolling balls of river mud
one by one, aligning each
as precisely as a mason,
layering all with grass
and the softness of down.

How delicate
these little mothers,
these winged creatures
who give up half a life
to nurture without promise
of success, with only blind faith
to lead them.

From their persistence
I take a lesson—
that one must go on
day after day,
keeping hope close,
laying bricks of mud and straw
one on top of another,
always believing in the vision
of a thousand souls rising
swift and sure and with rejoicing
toward heaven.

ON MARTRYDOM

He made a good garden, a wheat field, and later a farm…
beginning the construction of a chapel,
he laboring with his own hands…
Eusebio Kino recalling Father Francisco Saeta

Of his church, nothing remains,
nor of the garden that gave him
such delight. Of Saeta, my bright arrow,
all that is left is a box of bones and ash
weighing less than the weight of sorrow.

In my hands the truth of martyrdom—
charred bones pierced by arrows,
the ecstasy, if ecstasy there was,
negated by the cruelty of barbarians
in whom we placed our trust.

THE WHITE DOVE

In my youth I hoped to sacrifice self
for my faith. Now, with age heavy
on my shoulders, and many challenges
still before me, the words of our Lord
taste bitter on my lips.

Father forgive them,
for they know not
what they do.

At sunrise on April 2, 1695, the morning of Holy Saturday, forty
Tubutama Indians, angered at the cruelty of an Opata Indian overseer,
and, in their ignorance, supposing his cruelties to be condoned by the
Church, martyred Father Francisco Saeta at his mission in Caborca.
They burned his house and chapel, slaughtered cattle and horses, and
rode on to further plunder and revolt. Saeta, whose name in Latin
meant "arrow," was shot full of arrows and died holding his crucifix.
His body was burned. Only his bones were interred.

Although Father Kino wrote, "... his blood is glorious and most for-
tunate, since it was shed in the apostolic ministry," he also used the word
"barbarians," and I was forced to wonder what his true emotions were.

PASSAGES

> *The desert is mountains and wide valleys*
> *and the rain that does not come...*
> *The soul of the Cabeza Prieta is space and silence.*
> Chuck Bowden

Having crossed the desert
and returned so many times,
I find I have left part of myself there—
in the white heat
in the silence.

The mission garden welcomes me
with its green arms, yet there remains
a place within that has known
the invisible motion of mountains,
has walked the painted valleys
where antelope flow through brittle light
as if sand has become water.

Is this self-delusion
or the desert's trickery,
a spell cast, long as life
and irreversible?

I look out for answers
but find I cannot see.

LOAVES AND FISHES

We found bread, fresh and very good, which they baked for us
in the new oven I had ordered at San Xavier del Bac.
Eusebio Kino, 1697

Of fishes there are none, but here are loaves in plenty.
As the fragrance of new bread hovers on the desert air—
Bread baked in a round mud oven to my mother's recipe—
I reach back through years to the valley of my birth.

In winter, when the white wind blew and the mountains
hid their faces, the scent of her bread filled the house,
warmed even the pens where the goats, with their horizontal eyes,
were gestating lives that would arrive at the time of blossoms
and the snow melt that swelled the River Noce.

Here is the same creation, bread shaped by the hands
of women whose worn fingers seem those of my mother,
who sang as she kneaded the dough, who knew nothing more
than its rising for a reason she couldn't name.

Wheat, flour, water, women to give life,
women possessed of secrets lost in translation
but for their belief, their labor, the dancing motion
of their hands.

PART TWO: 1668-1700

CASA GRANDE

From a great distance
I glimpsed the city
rising from the river plain
like a mirage.

Riding closer, I found walls
without roofs,
windows with no one
looking out,

a city without children
or cooking fires,
a place empty of life
and laughter.

There was only silence,
for the walls could not speak
and even the cottonwood leaves
were mute.

I saw a tragedy unexplained,
perhaps an exodus
into slavery
or death.

Thus the importance of literacy,
of written histories.
Rome had her Virgil
and her Cicero,

Greece her Xenophon and Homer.
We have the words of Christ
recorded and passed down
through centuries.

In memory then of spirits lost,
I offered Mass so that the souls
of the departed might rest at last
in peace.

In 1694, Father Kino, having heard descriptions of Casa Grande, set out to see it for himself. Erroneously, he assumed it was one of the Seven Cities of Cibola, but then, as now, the ruins were both astonishing and mute.

INCREASE AND MULTIPLY

Be fruitful and multiply and replenish the earth.
                                                    Genesis

Here I oversee orchards, fields of wheat,
herds of cattle, and generations of new foals.
I supervise the stallion trumpeting
his fierce and natural desire.

There, and there, and there…
His duty finished, he rolls
in the sand, rises and trumpets
once again. I touch his muscled neck,
wet with the sweat of endeavor,
and am humbled by his honesty,

different from my own
but serving similar purpose.
Together we will multiply,
I by those I bring into the fold,
he by the magnificence of nature.

Which begs a question.

Is the horse not also touched by God,
and the bull, the ram, the ewe,
the seeds of wheat, corn, oats?
Is not this bounty evidence
of Other—the unknowable Divine,
a heart that beats within us all
even to the smallest...
a heart tumultuous,
resounding?

Eusebio Kino was one of the first to introduce stock breeding into Sonora and Arizona. He bred and supplied horses—particularly the Spanish Barbs, a strain of which is still being bred today—cattle, and sheep to all the missions under his direction, even shipping animals across the Gulf of California to missions there, yet another example of his extraordinary ability and intelligence.

FOSSIL

Here a leaf imprisoned in stone,
stem, fronds, veins tangible
as if etched in glass.

By what process
this immortality?
By what chance

of wind, rain, weather
can a leaf—one—
be rendered eternal?

My searching fingers
tell me neither means
nor chemistry,

only the fact of imprint
in perfect hieroglyphs.

SNAKE

Original sin... is the reverse side of creation.
Teilhard de Chardin

Surely Satan did not hide within this skin,
distort himself in sinuous obsidian
speckled gold and shining like sun on water.

Or perhaps he was more clever than I realize.
Perhaps he saw that Eve was lacking jewels,
a bracelet for her arm, glitter to satisfy
her need for recognition.

"Come," he said, all sibilance and temptation.
"Come." And it wasn't an apple he offered
but the treasure of himself as decoration
so she might preen and posture, tempt Adam

who was lost in Heaven's garden,
a useless soul without lust or calling,
bored, lacking form or purpose.

For where the challenge to his mind or loins,
where the call to being and triumph
in that place of absolute perfection?

And so I wonder, was it planned—
both by God and Satan—the loveliness,
the lure of difference, the strife
that presaged all our lives
as Eve and Adam plunged headfirst
from Paradise?

MONARCHS

They come! They come!
Light as lute music,
a multitude, a river
of painted wings.

They come! I do not know
from where, nor can I see
the destination of these scherzos
dancing on the air.

Like fallen leaves
they come to rest,
to sleep, to dream
here in the garden.

With stealth
I approach them,
hover, admire,
give thanks

for freedom, flight,
the joy that comes
with seeing
and with mystery,

for the suddenness
of love, its swift
embrace, a touch,
no more, of agony.

EVENSONG PIMERIA ALTA

The world here swallows the world,
and I am left with myself and the planet we call Earth.
                                    Chuck Bowden

I have followed a dove to this oasis,
the reverse of Noah, whose messenger
led him out of deluge to a mount
of rock and olives.

And yet the parallel remains,
for the desert stretches
like a living sea where I drift,
not without purpose
but directionless,

distracted by the last sunlight
reflected off a raven's wing
then pouring over steep
and empty slopes
with something like benevolence.

Evening is welcome here,
as welcome as water
or the trickery of light
mimicking rain.

Kneeling, I lift my face to heaven,
ask nothing more than what is given—
flights of doves, the springing of water
out of barren ground.

PART THREE

1700–1711

THE WHITE DOVE

I began also the very large church
of San Xavier del Bac, among the Sobaipuris.
Eusebio Kino, 1700

I will build a church here,
white-walled, with a bell
from Spain so finely cast
its music will strike echoes
from these black rock hills,
make ripples on the river's face.

I go out with spade and shovel,
take measurements in stubborn soil
and plant my cornerstones,
while around me doves,
the little ones on cautious feet,
stir the evening air with laughter.

Hoo hoo ... hoo hoo ... Quite possibly
I am the object of their mockery,
a man no longer young
but with a young man's dreams.
A collector of souls
turned architect of desire.
Oh, not the hunger of the flesh,
but simply for a place
I might call home.

(continued)

Is it arrogance to wish
a little room behind the baptistry
with books, a chair, a bed to lie on
after years of travel, long nights
spent on stony ground?

Am I selfish, foolish, useless
now that I am old and would possess
that which I gladly sacrificed
for my calling?

If so, in reparation, this church.
I dream it facing East
that the morning sun may enter
and touch all with its light.

That light which giveth joy to the world.

Eusebio Kino laid the cornerstones for the church of San Xavier del Bac, known as "The White Dove of the Desert," but he did not live to complete it. The current structure dates to 1783-1779, and was designed and completed by the Franciscan Fathers.

THE WHITE DOVE

WHO GUARDS ME WELL

October 6, 1700: We met the first Yumas…
They received us very affectionately, even giving the dog
which was with us water in a little basket, with all
kindness, as if he were a person, wondering that
he was so faithful, a thing never before seen by them.
Eusebio Kino

This supple hound,
this determined hunter,
trots in the shadow
cast by my horse,
asking no favors
but shade and friendship.

Ever the pragmatist,
he supplies his own supper,
rabbit, unwary bird,
lizards on lean days,
jerky from my hand.

Between us, respect.
I for his independence,
the purity of instinct,
his perfect symmetry.

(continued)

And he? He accepts me
as I am, companion traveler
who, like him, hungers,
thirsts, tastes the wind
and searches the horizon.

At night we rest, man and dog,
a habit from the fires of centuries.
We listen to the sounds
stirring the dark—
night birds calling, coyotes
in mad chorus, the serpent's
hushed but audible passage
through dried weeds.
Each protecting the other.

BLUE SHELLS

March 22, 1701: At midday I took the altitude
of the sun with the astrolabe and found that
this Gulf of California ended in 31 degrees latitude.
Eusebio Kino

A hundred leagues from the sea
I held its message in my hands.
Those blue husks that once protected life,
spoke of contiguity, a land undivided.

What scholar, scientist, priest can comprehend
the quick and startling light of intuition,
the intangible thrust of reason?

What mortal fail to marvel at the infinite —
earth's precise motion, the tide's turnings,
the sculpted pale perfection
of a simple shell?

Father Kino had long suspected that California was not, as was believed, an island, but a part of the American continent. When presented with a string of blue abalone shells by Yuma Indians, he made the connection with similar shells he'd observed during his time in Baja. From this, his deduction of a land route between Arizona, Sonora and Lower California, which he then, after many explorations, proved to his satisfaction.

LOOKING GLASS

Is this truly my face
looking back at me
from the water's surface?

Is it Kino—this countenance
withered like an aged apple,
brown-skinned as any Indian,

with grey painting
my beard, my hair,
the brows above my eyes?

The mirror does not lie,
nor the placid spring
that reflects me,

for, see, there is also sky,
the mountain bleached
by white sun into bone.

Though my heart beats
with a young man's fervor,
it seems I have grown old

here in this high desert place.
Old and, unlike Narcissus,
too homely for my own embrace.

THE WHITE DOVE

ON ARCHITECTURE
Mission San Ignacio De Caburica

No formidable granite here,
nor marble hewn from Cararra's heart.
No wondrous, painted dome
to draw our thoughts toward heaven.

Here, unadorned, four walls of earth
rise from the same earth
that fashioned them,
overhead a roof of trees
that once gave shelter to the small.

What dreamer of spires, arches,
patterned glass and opulence
would call this church
a fitting house for God?
What bold architect,
possessed of palatial visions,
admire our labors?

Possibly none.
Yet my very bones sing
with satisfaction.

(continued)

The moving sun paints white walls
with light and shadow.
A solitary dove has made her home
within a niche carved for a saint
who must, I fear, stand elsewhere.
And on the altar, the many-colored
unnamed flowers of the field
unfold in grace.

Who could wish for more?

The Lord dwells within us
and in all houses great or small.
I know this, as I know
that all the mighty monuments
to Him are less than this sweet peace,
this simple sanctuary.

THE WHITE DOVE

MUSIC LESSON

Today I am *Kappellmeister.*
Though they stumble over Latin,
my choir—ten ragged boys—
is enthralled by melody.
They mimic me as perfectly
as the mockingbirds
whose verbal repertoire
patterns our days.

Attuned to the singing of the world—
wind in the grass, the cornfields,
water flowing swiftly over stone,
and thunder's drum—
they make my task simple.

Perhaps it has always been thus,
with reason music's offspring,
not the reverse.
Intellect or instinct,
seen or unseen,
we believe.

Credo in unum Deum.

It is not impossible that Father Kino, as so many other missionaries, taught the singing of the Mass to his Indians. The use of the German, Kappellmeister, "choirmaster," would have come naturally to him as in his birthplace, Segno, both German and Italian were spoken, and he was, of course, educated in Austria and Germany.

IF I WERE

If I were other than I am,
priest, man of God,
I would worship still
the large things and the small,
the spill of pomegranates
over a rock wall,
the loveliness in every season,
spring to fall.

If I were painter
I would capture yellow leaves,
fading light, the deception
of a perfect fruit,
its treasure out of sight.

If I were wise
I'd know the reason
pain and joy
are often hidden,
understand the path
these flowers follow—
root to stem,
leaf to blossom,
orange, wind-tossed,
a flight of painted birds
worshipped, unbidden

BLUE LOBELIA, POPPIES, FILAREE

I come across them in unlikely places—
drifts of sand, among the rocks
in hardest soil—their subtle incense
sanctifying air.

It is the humblest flowers
that smell sweetest,
the insignificant, the small,
so valiant in fragility.

I must kneel to marvel,
stoop to find in each bright petal,
in every stem and minute leaf
the consummate prayer.

ALCHEMY

Aspen leaves have turned to gold,
the transmutation sought by sorcerers
for centuries.

Pity the alchemists their innocence,
their faith in spells, elixirs,
possibilities.

Pity the poverty of those lives
spent in darkness, the formula for release
elusive as wisdom or love

and as simple, though all answers,
once discerned, are simple. Only the path
is difficult,

the striving for that moment
when we divine that gold, like happiness,
cannot be summoned

but is where we find it—
in earth, mountains,
the dancing air.

PURE LOGIC

During the night, a snowfall.
Now the sun strikes fire
from earth's clean breast.

Newton's white light burns
my eyes with all the colors
of the spectrum, logic made visible,

proof, if proof be needed,
that purity is greater
than its parts,

that all the music
of the world can sing
within a flame.

Those who have seen fresh snow on the Catalina, Rincon, or Chiricahua Mountains have also seen perfect rainbows.

A BLESSING

Who is to say where they go, these creatures
of dust and filigree, their wings in tatters
yet durable enough to ride the air?

What miracle is this?
I ask in a voice soundless
as the flight of butterflies,
noiseless as light striking
the league-long cloud,

for miracle it is, this endless voyage
of those that might be called intangible,
so brief their rest, so empty the field,
when the wind has swept them away.

MEDITATIONS

Heron at mid-day
flows into
and out of
reflection.

All patterns
are endless.
All thoughts
one.

In this desert
life's thread spins out
in perfect solitude
with only the wind
and the raven's eye
to observe.

I remember storks
on widespread wings.
Now the song of cranes
touches my heart.

(continued)

From where these blue shells?
What mystery surrounds this land
that possesses me?

❧

Running antelope
lift the ground beneath their feet.
The sea rises....falls.

❧

In summer deluge
a million frogs are singing
hallelujah!

❧

STROLLING PLAYERS

How many nights have I lain awake and listened to their hallelujah
chorus, a clamor for life and a mate to share all with.
Jane Candia Coleman

All night the frogs on the river banks
strum and sing like viols
or the wind instruments
of itinerant Tyrolean players.

How often in my youth have I seen
those ragged men in tattered cloaks
piping and twanging in the town squares
simply for pleasure, or in celebration
of the harvest, or in funeral processions
winding their halting way to burial.

The hunchback bent over his pipes,
fingers fumbling for the plaintive notes
of sorrow; the drummer, gargoyle-faced,
beating time when there was no time left
for the dead.

(continued)

Up and up the steep trail—drummer, piper,
flautist—musicians of mortality
stepping to the beat of living hearts,
mourners marching toward finality,
and all the while the mountains
looking down God-like, their white faces
a mockery of grief.

Anyone living in the Southwest recognizes the singing of the frogs and toads that begins with the summer rains. Surely Father Kino heard them too, and perhaps recalled the processions of his childhood, the music of ragged local musicians echoing from the always snow-covered Alps.

It was on my trip through the Alto Adige that I, too, saw these musicians laboring up a steep track and following a coffin. The scene was Medieval, a Breughel painting come to life, a startling glimpse into another age that I have never forgotten.

THE WHITE DOVE

LITTLE BIRDS

So many
so quick
so small,

cloaked only
in feathers
and, perhaps,
in down.

You bless us
with music,
with the very fact
of being,

with your ability
to soar
beyond imagination
and all caring.

This morning
I scatter crumbs
from my breakfast
on barren earth,

(continued)

wait, watch
with hope
like a foretaste of joy
in my heart.

Come, little birds -
finches, sparrows,
top-notched quail
and unnamed others.

Come and feed,
a flock unlike the rest
but living, and with a duty
to perform.

TEMPORAL WISHES

Had I only a desk, steady
on hand-carved legs,
in place of these aged knees
that creak and groan
with the weight of years.

Had I only a book-filled room
alight with the voices of friends—
Descartes, Euclid, Eudoxis,
and blessed Augustine.

My fire burns to coals
as I crouch upon a rock
enumerating wishes—
tables, libraries, chests
of gold with which to build
my churches, give solace
where needed, bring faith
unwritten to this empty place
where my tablet's but a stretch
of sand, and all the wisdom
of the world is written by the stars.

EVENSONG MISSION DOLORES

Let there be no distinction between me
and words, between self and what is visible.
In the evening light I become all things—
wind, tossing leaves, a shower of birds
come to drink from sweet oases.

Let there be nothing that alters this place,
this garden shaped by love and duty,
intellect and the soul's need for order,
for out of order, justice takes its form.

My prayer tonight is simple,
my voice a slender reed
reaching timidly to heaven.
The earth is one, so let us all
grasp hands and sing
in magnificent chorus.

Our differences
are of man's making.
Our unity comes from above.
And so I beg a blessing…
that we may comprehend
Thy grace and it may touch our hearts
as does a rain of falling stars.

A MEETING

For how long has the hawk been perched,
motionless, on the fountain's edge,
feathers mimicking sun and shadow,
earth and air?

I, too, sit without moving,
my breath shallow,
my hands clasped
as if in prayer.

He stares at me from eyes
of fire-glazed stone,
priest and predator joined
for one fierce, glorious moment,

each begging release,
each demanding that
which is not ours to give—
self, and life, and function,

that power which determines purpose,
rules our faith and lifts us, wordless,
toward the light.

IN PERPETUAM

We who are childless by our calling
and our choice, give our names
to these brown-skinned children,
and we give them gladly,
not to perpetuate ourselves
but as a signature upon a document,
a stamp upon each baptized soul,
our names as bond.

List us: Mora, Campos, Leal,
Saeta, Gil, Ximeno, Gonsalvo,
Gonzales, Polici, Kino—
all of us have passed this way.

Our children are legion.

REVERIE

1. Magdalena, Mexico, March, 1711

The one certainty in my life
aside from purpose
has been migration.
Much as the cranes, the butterflies,
I move with the wind of necessity,
always aware of the intangible voice
that beckons, and I go,
not on transparent wings,
though I wish it were so,
but mounted on the bony ridge
of a black mule's back.

My path has never been straight,
my route one of detours.
In this I mimic life,
that lonely journey
of dedication, inspired choice.

2. Val Di Non, Italy, 1662

How slowly the old mule walked!
Dust rose from under his hooves
and hung around us like a veil
through which the road beckoned
with all the intent of a young
and desirable girl,
and my blood quickened,
my heart flew before me,
the taste of the future ripe
in my mouth like chestnuts
or new wine.

(continued)

Turning, I looked back at Segno,
at the road that wound like a string
down the mountain where, in spring,
the apples cast their petals everywhere.

I waved and said farewell,
followed the river toward Trento,
town of antiquity and holy Council,
seat of learning to which I would never return.

From there I followed the route of Hannibal
whose elephants challenged those formidable heights,
and as I went, I dreamed a young man's dreams.
Carthaginian, knight, Crusader armed with God's word,
I flew toward my destiny, while the old mule plodded on,
uncaring.

3. *The Jesuit College, Hala, Austria, 1663*

Death held no rewards. Not for a young man
with a young man's fervor. *Give me life!*
The plea caught in my throat
as I fought the darkness.

God, give me life! And it was given
after all hope was given up.
I pledged my sacred oath to heaven,
willed my worldly goods to God;
the church, the sacred Order,
and then awoke into a different dream.
I am in it still.

4. Mexico, 1681

In those first days I longed for China,
land of mathematics, maps, and martyrs.
The East possessed my dreams,
became the place where I would make
the greatest sacrifice, my life, for my belief.
But God decreed other.

In a gamble, fool's play,
I drew lots and lost my hopes
of glory, death, a place,
however small, in history.

Humbled, Mexico surrounded me
with light and shadow, drought and thorns,
dark-eyed wary people I now care for as my own.

For them, for God, I have traveled the missions
that spread like a rosary of strange names
in even stranger places—Cocospera,
Tubutama, Tumacacori, Guevavi, Bac—
each my home for a night, a day,
each a place of temporary rest.
Each a flower where I flutter down,
sip the blood of Christ,
and gain the strength to go forth
again, and again, and again.

(continued)

5. Magdalena, Mexico, 1711

Sanctus, Sanctus, Sanctus.
Around me earth spirals
into light and distance,
great rivers run to the sea,
and always, somewhere,
dark heads bowed in prayer.

So many journeys.
So many vanished years.

I raise the Host
and once again offer myself
with a love beyond all love.

Oh, Lord, I hear.
I come.

Taken ill while celebrating a Mass in dedication of a new mission chapel, Father Eusebio Kino, S.J., died in Magdalena, Mexico in 1711 and was buried there. His actual grave was sought for many years, but was not found until 1966.

THE WHITE DOVE

Suggested Reading

For those wishing to read more about the extraordinary life and accomplishments of Father Kino, I recommend the following:

Bannon, John Francis. *Herbert Eugene Bolton, the Historian and the Man.* Tucson: University of Arizona Press, 1978.

Bolton, Herbert Eugene. *Kino's Historical Memoir of Pimeria Alta.* Berkeley, California: University of California Press, 1948.

Bolton, Herbert Eugene. *The Rim of Christendom.* Tucson: University of Arizona Press, 1984.

Bowden, Chuck. "Desert Wilderness." *Arizona Highways* (January 2003).

Clevenger, Ben. *The Far Side of the Sea.* Tucson: The Jesuit Fathers of Southern Arizona, 2003.

De Grazia, Ted. Introduction by Patricia P. Paylore, with paintings by DeGrazia. *De Grazia and Padre Kino.* Tucson: DeGrazia Gallery of the Sun, 1979.

Morgan, Richard J. Jr. *A Guide to Historic Missions and Churches of the Arizona-Sonora Borderlands.* Solola, Guatemala: Adventures in Education, 1995.

Polzer, Charles W., S.J. *Kino—A Legacy.* Tucson: Jesuit Fathers of Southern Arizona, 1998.

Smith, Fay Jackson, John L. Kessell, and Francis J. Fox, S.J. *Father Kino in Arizona.* Phoenix: Arizona Historical Foundation, 1966.

I recommend visiting the DeGrazia Gallery and, of course, the Mission of San Xavier del Bac, the "White Dove of the Desert," south of Tucson.

JANE CANDIA COLEMAN is the recipient of three Western Heritage Awards from the National Cowboy Museum & Western Heritage Center for two collections of poetry, *No Roof But Sky* and *The Red Drum* (High Plains Press), and a collection of short fiction, *Stories From Mesa Country* (Ohio University Press). Her work has received two Spur Awards from Western Writers of America. Her memoir, *Mountain Time*, was a finalist for the Willa Award from Women Writing the West, as was her historical novel, *Matchless*. *Tombstone Travesty* received the Willa Award for best historical novel in 2004.

Coleman is fiction mentor in Carlow University's MFA Program. A five-time Pulitzer nominee, she lives and writes in Tucson, Arizona where the "White Dove of the Desert," the San Xavier del Bac Mission, is located.

The text is eleven-point Berkeley Oldstyle Book
by the International Type Company.
Display type is Cyan by the Wilton Foundry and Missale AS Incana.
The book is printed on
fifty-five pound Nature's Natural,
a fifty percent post consumer recycled paper, processed acid free,
by Thomson-Shore

green
press
INITIATIVE

High Plains Press is committed to preserving ancient forests and
natural resources. We elected to print *The White Dove* on 50% post
consumer recycled paper, processed chlorine free. As a result, for
this printing, we have saved:

3 Trees (40' Tall and 6-8" Diameter)
1,358 Gallons of Wastewater
546 Kilowatt Hours of Electricity
150 Pounds of Solid Waste
294 Pounds of Greenhouse Gases

High Plains Press made this paper choice because our printer,
Thomson-Shore, Inc., is a member of Green Press Initiative, a
nonprofit program dedicated to supporting authors, publishers, and
suppliers in their efforts to reduce their use of fiber obtained from
endangered forests.

For more information, visit www.greenpressinitiative.org